Growing Orchids Simple Guide for Beginners

Knowing the Importance of Orchids

By

Braxton Orlan

Table of Contents

CHAPTER 1

Introduction to Orchids

1.1 What Are Orchids?

Orchids, scientifically known as Orchidaceae, constitute one of the largest and most diverse families of flowering plants, with over 25,000 documented species found across every continent except Antarctica. Renowned for their exquisite beauty, captivating fragrances, and intricate structures, orchids hold a special place in the hearts of botanists, horticulturists, and enthusiasts alike.

At the heart of what makes orchids truly remarkable is their remarkable diversity. Orchids exhibit an astonishing array of shapes, sizes, colors, and patterns, ranging from the delicate miniature blooms of the Pleurothallis genus to the large, flamboyant flowers of the Cattleya species. This diversity has led to orchids occupying a wide range of ecological niches, from the tropical rainforests to the arid deserts, and from the mountainous regions to the coastal plains.

Orchids are characterized by their unique reproductive structures, which set them apart from other flowering plants. Unlike typical flowers with five petals, orchids typically have three petals and three sepals, with one petal often highly modified into a distinct shape known as the lip or labellum. This lip serves as a landing platform for pollinators, such as bees, butterflies, moths, and birds, facilitating the transfer of pollen from one flower to another.

Another fascinating aspect of orchids is their remarkable adaptability and evolutionary strategies for pollination. Many orchids have co-evolved with specific pollinators, developing elaborate mechanisms to ensure successful pollination. Some orchids mimic the appearance and scent of female insects to attract male pollinators, while others employ intricate traps to capture and transfer pollen onto visiting insects.

Beyond their ecological significance, orchids have held cultural and symbolic importance throughout history. Revered for their beauty and rarity, orchids have been revered in various cultures as symbols of love, luxury, fertility, and elegance. In ancient civilizations such as Greece and China, orchids were associated with virility and were believed to possess aphrodisiac properties. In Victorian England, orchid collecting became a fashionable hobby among the elite, leading to orchids being regarded as symbols of refinement and prestige.

Today, orchids continue to captivate and inspire people around the world. Whether admired in their natural habitats, cultivated in botanical gardens, or cherished in private collections, orchids serve as a reminder of the boundless wonders of the natural world. With their unparalleled beauty, intricate biology, and rich cultural history, orchids truly deserve their reputation as the jewels of the plant kingdom.

1.2 History and Significance

The history and significance of orchids trace back millennia, intertwining with the cultural, economic, and scientific narratives of civilizations around the globe. Orchids have fascinated humanity since ancient times, leaving an indelible mark on art, literature, medicine, and commerce.

Ancient civilizations revered orchids for their beauty and perceived mystical properties. In ancient Greece, orchids were associated with fertility and were believed to be symbols of virility. Greek scholars such as Theophrastus and Dioscorides documented orchids in their botanical writings, laying the foundation for the scientific study of these enigmatic plants.

During the age of exploration in the 17th and 18th centuries, European explorers encountered exotic orchids in distant lands, particularly in tropical regions such as Asia, Africa, and the Americas. Orchid fever gripped Europe, leading to a surge in orchid collecting and trade. Wealthy collectors spared no expense in acquiring rare and exotic orchids, fueling a craze known as orchidelirium.

Orchids became prized possessions among the European elite, symbolizing wealth, refinement, and sophistication. Orchid collectors established extravagant orchid houses and conservatories to showcase their prized specimens, with some orchids fetching exorbitant prices at auctions.

The Victorian era saw orchids reach the height of their popularity, with orchid cultivation becoming a fashionable pursuit among the aristocracy. Orchid societies and clubs proliferated, providing platforms for enthusiasts to exchange knowledge, share cultivation techniques, and showcase their prized blooms. Orchid competitions became prestigious events, with growers vying for coveted awards and accolades.

Orchids also played a significant role in the field of science, capturing the attention of botanists, taxonomists, and researchers. Charles Darwin, the renowned naturalist, was fascinated by the intricate adaptations of orchids for pollination, which he described in his seminal work "On the Origin of Species."

In the 19th and 20th centuries, advances in botanical exploration, taxonomy, and horticulture led to the discovery of thousands of new orchid species and the development of hybridization techniques. Orchid breeding became a specialized art form, resulting in an explosion of new orchid cultivars with a diverse range of colors, shapes, and fragrances.

1.3 Why Grow Orchids?

The decision to grow orchids is motivated by a myriad of reasons, ranging from their exquisite beauty to the satisfaction derived from nurturing these fascinating plants. Below are several compelling reasons why individuals choose to cultivate orchids:

1. Beauty: Orchids are renowned for their stunning and diverse array of flowers, which come in a multitude of shapes, sizes, colors, and patterns. From delicate miniature blooms to

large, flamboyant flowers, orchids captivate the imagination with their unparalleled beauty. Growing orchids allows enthusiasts to surround themselves with these living works of art, enhancing the aesthetic appeal of homes, gardens, and indoor spaces.

2. Diversity: Orchids constitute one of the largest and most diverse families of flowering plants, with over 25,000 documented species found in virtually every corner of the globe. This remarkable diversity offers endless possibilities for orchid enthusiasts, who can explore and cultivate a wide range of species and hybrids, each with its unique characteristics and growing requirements.

3. Challenge and Reward: Orchid cultivation presents a rewarding challenge for hobbyists and gardening enthusiasts. Unlike traditional houseplants, orchids often require specialized care and

attention, including precise watering, lighting, and temperature conditions. Successfully cultivating orchids requires patience, experimentation, and continuous learning, making it a deeply rewarding and intellectually stimulating hobby.

4. Therapeutic Benefits: Growing orchids can be a therapeutic and stress-relieving activity, providing individuals with a sense of fulfillment and relaxation. Tending to orchids encourages mindfulness and connection with nature, offering a welcome respite from the stresses of modern life. Additionally, caring for orchids fosters a sense of responsibility and nurturing, promoting emotional well-being and personal growth.

5. Educational Opportunities: Orchid cultivation offers numerous educational opportunities for enthusiasts of all ages. Studying orchids allows individuals to learn about botany, ecology, and plant

physiology, deepening their understanding of the natural world. Orchid enthusiasts can also participate in workshops, seminars, and botanical tours, expanding their knowledge and connecting with fellow enthusiasts.

6. Community and Camaraderie: Orchid cultivation fosters a sense of community and camaraderie among enthusiasts, who often come together to share knowledge, experiences, and resources. Orchid societies, clubs, and online forums provide platforms for enthusiasts to exchange tips, troubleshoot problems, and showcase their prized blooms. Participating in the orchid community allows individuals to forge friendships, build networks, and enrich their orchid-growing journey.

7. Conservation: Many orchid enthusiasts are passionate about orchid conservation and preservation efforts. As habitat destruction, climate change, and illegal trade

threaten wild orchid populations, cultivating orchids plays a vital role in safeguarding endangered species and promoting biodiversity. By growing orchids responsibly and supporting conservation initiatives, enthusiasts contribute to the protection of these precious plants for future generations.

The decision to grow orchids is motivated by a combination of factors, including their beauty, diversity, challenge, therapeutic benefits, educational opportunities, community engagement, and conservation significance. Whether driven by a love for nature, a desire for personal enrichment, or a commitment to environmental stewardship, cultivating orchids offers a deeply fulfilling and rewarding experience for enthusiasts of all backgrounds and interests.

CHAPTER 2

Understanding Orchids

2.1 Anatomy of an Orchid

Understanding the anatomy of an orchid is essential for successful cultivation and appreciation of these fascinating plants. While orchids exhibit a wide range of shapes, sizes, and structures, they share several key anatomical features that distinguish them from other flowering plants:

1. Roots: Orchids possess specialized roots adapted to their epiphytic or terrestrial lifestyles. These roots serve multiple functions, including anchoring the plant, absorbing water and nutrients, and photosynthesis. Orchid roots often possess a spongy outer layer known as velamen, which helps them absorb moisture from the environment.

2. Pseudobulbs: Some orchid species produce pseudobulbs, swollen stem structures that store water and nutrients. Pseudobulbs serve as reservoirs during periods of drought or nutrient scarcity, enabling orchids to survive in challenging environments. Examples of orchids with pseudobulbs include Cattleya, Oncidium, and Dendrobium species.

3. Leaves: Orchid leaves vary widely in shape, size, and texture, reflecting adaptations to different growing conditions. In epiphytic orchids, leaves are often thick, fleshy, and adapted to retain moisture, while terrestrial orchids may have thinner leaves adapted to photosynthesis and gas exchange. Orchid leaves may also exhibit specialized structures such as pseudobulbs or aerial roots.

4. Flowers: Orchid flowers are renowned for their exquisite beauty and complex structures. Orchid flowers typically consist of three sepals and three petals, with one

petal highly modified into a lip or labellum. The lip serves as a landing platform for pollinators and often features intricate patterns, colors, and fragrances to attract them. Orchid flowers may vary in size, shape, color, and scent, depending on the species and hybridization.

5. Inflorescence: Orchid flowers are borne on specialized reproductive structures known as inflorescences or flower spikes. Inflorescences can take various forms, including racemes, panicles, spikes, or umbels, depending on the orchid species. Some orchids produce solitary flowers, while others form clusters or sprays of blooms.

6. Reproductive Organs: Orchids possess unique reproductive organs adapted for specialized pollination mechanisms. The male reproductive organ, called the column, contains the pollen-producing anther and the sticky stigma, where pollinia or pollinaria are deposited. Pollinaria

are often enclosed within protective structures known as pollinia or pollinia.

2.2 Different Types of Orchids

Orchids are incredibly diverse, with thousands of species and hybrids encompassing a wide range of shapes, sizes, colors, and growing habits. While it's impossible to cover every type of orchid in detail, below are some broad categories that highlight the diversity within the Orchidaceae family:

1. Phalaenopsis Orchids: Phalaenopsis, or moth orchids, are among the most popular and widely cultivated orchids worldwide. Known for their elegant, arching sprays of flowers and long-lasting blooms, Phalaenopsis orchids are prized for their ease of care and adaptability to indoor environments.

2. Cattleya Orchids: Cattleya orchids
    are renowned for their large, showy
    flowers and intoxicating fragrances.
    Often referred to as "queen of the
    orchids," Cattleyas come in a myriad
    of colors and patterns, ranging from
    vibrant purples and pinks to soft
    pastels and pure whites.

3. Dendrobium Orchids: Dendrobium
    orchids encompass a diverse group
    of species characterized by their
    cane-like or sympodial growth
    habits. Dendrobiums produce
    clusters of colorful flowers along the
    length of their stems, with some
    species blooming profusely once a
    year, while others bloom multiple
    times throughout the year.

4. Oncidium Orchids: Oncidium
    orchids, commonly known as
    "dancing lady" orchids, are
    celebrated for their cascading sprays
    of small, brightly colored flowers.
    Oncidiums exhibit a wide range of
    growth habits, from compact
    miniatures to sprawling epiphytes,

making them versatile additions to orchid collections.

5. Paphiopedilum Orchids: Paphiopedilum, or slipper orchids, are prized for their unique pouch-like flowers and mottled foliage. Unlike most orchids, Paphiopedilums grow terrestrially or lithophytically, often in leaf litter or rocky habitats. Their exotic appearance and ease of care make them popular choices for indoor cultivation.

6. Vanda Orchids: Vanda orchids are beloved for their vibrant colors, long-lasting blooms, and graceful, pendulous growth habits. Vandas produce large, flat flowers in a wide range of hues, including blues, purples, pinks, and oranges. With their aerial root system and preference for bright, indirect light, Vandas thrive in hanging baskets or mounted on driftwood.

These are just a few examples of the diverse array of orchids available to growers. Within each broad category, there are countless species, hybrids, and cultivars, each with its unique characteristics and growing requirements. Whether you're drawn to the delicate beauty of Phalaenopsis, the flamboyant blooms of Cattleyas, or the exotic allure of Paphiopedilums, there's an orchid to suit every taste and growing environment. Exploring the world of orchids is a rewarding journey filled with discovery, beauty, and endless possibilities.

2.3 Orchid Habitats

Orchids are renowned for their remarkable ability to adapt to diverse habitats, ranging from tropical rainforests to arid deserts and temperate woodlands. Understanding the natural habitats of orchids is crucial for successful cultivation and conservation efforts. Below are some of the key habitats where orchids thrive:

1. Tropical Rainforests: Tropical rainforests are among the richest and most biodiverse ecosystems on the

planet, providing ideal habitats for a vast array of orchid species. Orchids in tropical rainforests often grow as epiphytes, clinging to trees and branches, where they receive filtered light, ample moisture, and nutrients from decomposing organic matter. Examples of orchids found in tropical rainforests include Phalaenopsis, Dendrobium, and Vanda species.

2. Cloud Forests: Cloud forests, also known as montane or mossy forests, are characterized by their persistent mist and fog, which create cool, humid conditions ideal for orchid growth. Orchids in cloud forests often inhabit tree branches, moss-covered rocks, and forest floors, where they benefit from high humidity and diffused light. Species such as Masdevallia, Dracula, and Pleurothallis thrive in cloud forest habitats, producing exquisite blooms adapted to cooler temperatures.

3. Dry Forests and Scrublands: Orchids
    can also be found in drier habitats
    such as dry forests, scrublands, and
    savannas, where they exhibit
    adaptations to withstand periods of
    drought and high temperatures. In
    these habitats, orchids may grow
    terrestrially or lithophytically, often
    in the shelter of shrubs, rocks, or
    cacti. Examples of orchids adapted to
    dry habitats include members of the
    genus Catasetum, Epidendrum, and
    Laelia.

4. Coastal Environments: Orchids are
    well-adapted to coastal
    environments, where they tolerate
    salty air, fluctuating temperatures,
    and sandy or rocky substrates.
    Coastal orchids often grow in dunes,
    mangrove forests, and rocky cliffs,
    where they benefit from abundant
    sunlight and periodic salt spray.
    Orchids such as Encyclia tampensis,
    Habenaria repens, and Vanilla
    barbellata are examples of species
    found in coastal habitats.

5. Seasonally Dry Forests: Orchids inhabit seasonally dry forests, where they experience distinct wet and dry seasons. During the wet season, orchids absorb moisture from rainfall and dew, while during the dry season, they may enter a period of dormancy or rely on stored water reserves. Orchids in seasonally dry forests may grow as epiphytes, lithophytes, or terrestrials, depending on the availability of water and nutrients. Examples of orchids found in seasonally dry forests include Cattleya, Oncidium, and Encyclia species.

6. Temperate Woodlands: Orchids also thrive in temperate woodlands and forests, where they often grow as terrestrial or saprophytic species. In temperate regions, orchids may bloom in spring or summer, producing delicate flowers adapted to cooler temperatures. Orchids such as Cypripedium (Lady's Slipper orchids), Calypso, and Pleione are

examples of species found in
temperate woodlands.

CHAPTER 3

Getting Started

3.1 Selecting Orchids

Selecting the right orchids for your growing conditions and preferences is crucial for a successful and rewarding orchid-growing experience. With thousands of species and hybrids available, choosing the perfect orchids can be both exciting and overwhelming. Here are some factors to consider when selecting orchids:

1. Growing Environment: Assess your growing environment, including light levels, temperature, humidity, and available space. Different orchid species have specific requirements, so it's essential to choose orchids that thrive in your conditions. For example, if you have bright, indirect light, consider orchids such as Phalaenopsis, Paphiopedilum, or Dendrobium, which are well-suited

to indoor environments. If you have a greenhouse or outdoor space with ample sunlight, you may opt for orchids like Cattleya, Vanda, or Oncidium, which require brighter light levels.

2. Skill Level: Consider your level of experience and expertise in orchid cultivation. Some orchids are more forgiving and easier to care for, making them ideal choices for beginners. Look for orchids with straightforward care requirements, such as Phalaenopsis, Paphiopedilum, or Oncidium hybrids. As you gain confidence and experience, you can explore more challenging orchid species and hybrids with specialized care needs.

3. Bloom Time and Duration: Determine your preferences regarding bloom time and duration. Some orchids bloom seasonally, producing flowers once or twice a year, while others bloom continuously or sporadically

throughout the year. Consider whether you prefer orchids with long-lasting blooms or those that bloom prolifically but briefly. Orchids such as Phalaenopsis and Cattleya hybrids are known for their long-lasting flowers, while Dendrobium and Oncidium hybrids often produce profuse blooms in shorter bursts.

4. Fragrance and Aesthetic Appeal: Take into account the fragrance and aesthetic appeal of orchids when making your selection. Orchids come in a wide range of colors, shapes, sizes, and fragrances, allowing you to choose varieties that complement your personal taste and decor. Whether you prefer vibrant colors, delicate pastels, or striking patterns, there's an orchid to suit every aesthetic preference. Additionally, consider the fragrance of orchids, as some species produce intoxicating scents that enhance the sensory experience.

5. Availability and Source: Research reputable orchid vendors, nurseries, or online retailers that offer high-quality orchids and provide reliable information and customer support. Attend orchid shows, exhibitions, or sales events to explore a wide selection of orchids and interact with knowledgeable growers and vendors. Consider purchasing orchids from reputable sources that prioritize plant health, ethical practices, and customer satisfaction.

6. Personal Preferences and Goals: Ultimately, choose orchids that resonate with your personal preferences, interests, and goals. Whether you're drawn to species orchids, hybrid orchids, miniature orchids, or fragrant orchids, follow your instincts and select orchids that inspire joy and passion. Consider your long-term goals for orchid cultivation, whether it's building a diverse collection, participating in

orchid shows, or breeding new hybrids.

By carefully considering these factors and doing thorough research, you can select orchids that are well-suited to your growing conditions, skill level, preferences, and goals. Remember that orchid cultivation is a journey of learning and discovery, so don't be afraid to experiment, make mistakes, and learn from experience. With patience, dedication, and a passion for orchids, you can create a vibrant and rewarding orchid collection that brings beauty and joy into your life.

3.2 Essential Equipment and Supplies

To embark on a successful journey of orchid cultivation, it's essential to have the right equipment and supplies on hand. Here's a list of essential items you'll need to care for your orchids effectively:

1. Pots or Containers: Choose pots or containers suitable for the specific needs of your orchids. Opt for pots with drainage holes to prevent waterlogged roots and promote healthy root growth. Transparent or semi-transparent pots are ideal for orchids with photosynthetic roots, allowing light to reach the roots and promoting photosynthesis.

2. Growing Medium: Select a suitable growing medium tailored to the requirements of your orchids. Common orchid growing mediums include orchid bark, sphagnum moss, coconut husk chips, perlite, and charcoal. Choose a well-draining medium that provides adequate aeration and moisture retention for healthy root growth.

3. Fertilizer: Invest in a balanced orchid fertilizer formulated specifically for orchids. Choose a fertilizer with a balanced N-P-K ratio (nitrogen, phosphorus, potassium) and essential micronutrients. Follow the

manufacturer's instructions for dilution and frequency of application, and avoid overfertilizing, which can lead to salt buildup and root damage.

4. Watering Can or Sprayer: Use a watering can with a fine rose or a handheld sprayer to water your orchids gently and evenly. Avoid using a hose or watering can with a strong stream, as it can damage delicate orchid roots and foliage.

5. pH Meter: Consider investing in a pH meter to monitor the pH level of your watering solution and growing medium. Orchids prefer slightly acidic to neutral pH levels (pH 5.5-6.5), so adjust your watering and fertilizing practices accordingly.

6. Humidity Tray or Humidifier: Maintain adequate humidity levels for your orchids, especially if you're growing them indoors or in dry climates. Place orchids on humidity trays filled with water and pebbles or

use a humidifier to increase humidity around your plants.

7. Pruning Shears or Scissors: Keep a pair of sharp pruning shears or scissors handy for pruning dead or damaged roots, flowers, or foliage. Sterilize your pruning tools before and after each use to prevent the spread of diseases and infections.

8. Support Stakes or Clips: Provide support for tall or top-heavy orchid spikes by using support stakes, clips, or bamboo skewers. Gently secure the spikes to the stakes to prevent them from bending or breaking under the weight of the flowers.

9. Pest Control Products: Be prepared to deal with common orchid pests such as aphids, mealybugs, scale insects, and spider mites. Keep insecticidal soap, neem oil, or other organic pest control products on hand to treat infestations promptly.

10. Potting Bench or Work Area: Set up a dedicated potting bench or work area for repotting and grooming your orchids. Keep your tools, supplies, and equipment organized and easily accessible for convenience.

By having these essential equipment and supplies on hand, you'll be well-equipped to care for your orchids and create an optimal growing environment for healthy growth and blooming.

3.3 Choosing the Right Growing Medium

Selecting the right growing medium is crucial for orchid cultivation, as it provides support, aeration, moisture retention, and nutrient uptake for healthy root growth. There are several types of growing mediums commonly used for orchids, each with its unique characteristics and suitability for different orchid species and growing conditions. Here are some popular options:

1. Orchid Bark: Orchid bark is one of the most widely used growing mediums for orchids, particularly epiphytic species. Orchid bark is made from the bark of various tree species, such as fir, pine, or cedar, and comes in different sizes, grades, and compositions. Choose a medium-grade orchid bark with large chunks for orchids with robust root systems, and fine-grade orchid bark for smaller or more delicate roots.

2. Sphagnum Moss: Sphagnum moss is a natural, organic growing medium prized for its moisture retention properties. It's commonly used for orchids that require high humidity, such as Phalaenopsis and Paphiopedilum species. When using sphagnum moss, ensure it's fresh, clean, and free from contaminants to prevent mold or bacterial growth.

3. Coconut Husk Chips: Coconut husk chips, also known as coco chips or coir, are derived from the outer husk of coconuts. Coconut husk chips

provide excellent drainage, aeration, and moisture retention, making them suitable for a wide range of orchids. They're especially popular for orchids with coarse or robust root systems, such as Cattleya and Dendrobium species.

4. Perlite: Perlite is a lightweight, volcanic rock material commonly used as a component in orchid potting mixes. Perlite improves drainage, aeration, and moisture retention when mixed with other growing mediums such as orchid bark or sphagnum moss. It's particularly useful for orchids that prefer a more open and airy growing environment, such as Oncidium and Epidendrum species.

5. Charcoal: Charcoal, or horticultural charcoal, is often added to orchid potting mixes to improve drainage and prevent odors and rot. Charcoal helps absorb excess moisture and impurities, promoting a healthy root environment for orchids. It's

especially beneficial for orchids grown in humid or tropical climates, where root rot and fungal diseases may be a concern.

When choosing a growing medium for your orchids, consider factors such as the orchid species, growing environment, watering frequency, and cultural preferences. Experiment with different combinations and proportions of growing mediums to find the optimal mix for your orchids' needs. Remember to repot your orchids every 1-2 years to refresh the growing medium and ensure continued healthy growth and blooming.

CHAPTER 4

Orchid Care Basics

4.1 Light Requirements

Understanding the light requirements of orchids is essential for their health, growth, and blooming. Proper light exposure influences photosynthesis, flower production, and overall plant vigor. Different orchid species have varying light preferences, so it's crucial to match their needs with the appropriate light conditions. Here's a guide to understanding orchid light requirements:

1. Light Intensity: Orchids require adequate light to thrive, but the intensity of light they prefer varies depending on their natural habitat. Generally, orchids can be categorized into three light categories based on their light requirements:

- High Light: Orchids in this category require bright, indirect light or direct sunlight for several hours each day. Examples include Vanda, Cattleya, and Dendrobium species. These orchids typically have thick, leathery leaves and can tolerate more intense light levels.

- Medium Light: Orchids in this category prefer moderate to bright, indirect light, but may benefit from some protection from direct sunlight during the hottest part of the day. Examples include Phalaenopsis, Oncidium, and Miltonia species. These orchids have thinner leaves and can tolerate lower light levels.

- Low Light: Orchids in this category thrive in low to moderate light conditions, such as shaded areas or north-facing windows. Examples include Paphiopedilum, Phragmipedium, and Masdevallia species. These orchids have adapted to low light levels in their natural habitats and may burn or wilt if exposed to direct sunlight.

2. Light Duration: Orchids require a balance of light and darkness to maintain healthy growth cycles. Provide orchids with 10-14 hours of light each day during the growing season to promote vegetative growth and flower development. During the rest period or dormancy phase, reduce light exposure to 8-10 hours per day to simulate natural conditions and encourage blooming.

3. Light Quality: Orchids benefit from full-spectrum light sources that provide a balanced mix of wavelengths, including red, blue, and white light. Natural sunlight is the

best source of light for orchids, but artificial grow lights can be used to supplement or augment natural light, especially in indoor environments with limited sunlight exposure. Choose grow lights with a color temperature of 5000-6500 Kelvin (K) for optimal plant growth and flowering.

4. Light Distance: Position orchids at the appropriate distance from light sources to prevent sunburn or heat stress. Place high-light orchids closer to windows or grow lights to maximize light exposure, but avoid direct sunlight during the hottest part of the day to prevent leaf damage. Medium-light and low-light orchids can be placed further away from light sources to avoid burning or overheating.

5. Light Adjustment: Monitor orchids regularly for signs of light stress or inadequate light exposure, such as yellowing or bleaching of leaves, elongated growth, or failure to

bloom. Adjust the positioning of orchids or the intensity of light sources as needed to provide optimal light conditions. Rotate orchids periodically to ensure even light distribution and balanced growth.

4.2 Temperature and Humidity

Temperature and humidity play crucial roles in the health and well-being of orchids, as they influence growth, blooming, and overall plant vigor. Different orchid species have specific temperature and humidity requirements, so it's essential to understand and provide optimal conditions for your orchids. Here's a guide to orchid temperature and humidity requirements:

1. Temperature:

    - Orchids originate from diverse habitats ranging from tropical rainforests to temperate woodlands, so their temperature preferences vary accordingly.

- Most orchids thrive in temperatures ranging from 60°F to 80°F (15°C to 27°C) during the day and slightly cooler temperatures at night. However, specific orchid species may have narrower temperature ranges or unique temperature preferences.

- Provide adequate ventilation and air circulation around orchids to prevent heat buildup and maintain optimal temperature levels. Use fans or open windows to promote airflow, especially during hot and humid weather.

2. Day-Night Temperature Differential:

- Mimic natural temperature fluctuations by providing a day-night temperature differential, which helps stimulate growth, flowering, and overall plant health.

- Aim for a temperature drop of 10°F to 15°F (5°C to 8°C) between day and night temperatures, as this simulates the conditions orchids experience in their native habitats.

- Use thermostats or temperature monitors to monitor temperature fluctuations and adjust heating or cooling systems as needed to maintain optimal conditions.

3. Humidity:

- Orchids thrive in environments with moderate to high humidity levels, typically ranging from 50% to 80% relative humidity.

- Maintain adequate humidity levels by using humidity

trays, humidifiers, or
grouping orchids together to
create microclimates with
higher humidity.

- Avoid placing orchids near
drafts, heaters, or air
conditioners, as these can
create dry air and reduce
humidity levels around the
plants.

- Monitor humidity levels
regularly using hygrometers
or humidity meters and adjust
humidity-enhancing
measures as needed to
provide optimal conditions.

4. Terrariums and Enclosures:

- Consider growing humidity-
loving orchids in terrariums,
enclosed glass containers, or
humidity chambers to create
controlled environments with
high humidity levels.

- Terrariums provide a stable microclimate with consistent temperature and humidity levels, ideal for orchids such as jewel orchids (Ludisia discolor) or miniature orchids.

Maintaining optimal temperature and humidity levels is essential for promoting healthy growth, flowering, and overall well-being of orchids. By understanding your orchids' temperature and humidity requirements and providing appropriate environmental conditions, you can cultivate thriving orchid plants that reward you with beautiful blooms and lush foliage.

4.3 Watering Techniques

Proper watering is crucial for the health and vitality of orchids, as it ensures adequate hydration while preventing issues such as root rot, dehydration, and nutrient deficiencies. Different orchid species have specific watering requirements based on their natural habitats, so it's essential to understand and implement appropriate watering techniques. Here's a guide to orchid watering techniques:

1. Frequency:

    - Orchid watering frequency depends on factors such as the orchid species, growing medium, environmental conditions, and time of year.

    - In general, most orchids prefer to dry out slightly between waterings, so avoid overwatering by allowing the growing medium to dry out partially before watering again.

    - Water orchids more frequently during the active growing season (spring and summer) when they're actively producing new growth and flowering. Reduce watering frequency during the rest period or dormancy phase (fall and winter) to mimic natural seasonal fluctuations.

2. Water Quality:

   - Use clean, filtered water or rainwater whenever possible to avoid mineral buildup, salts, or contaminants that can harm orchids' sensitive roots.

   - If using tap water, allow it to sit for 24 hours to allow chlorine and other chemicals to dissipate before watering orchids.

3. Watering Method:

   - Water orchids thoroughly, ensuring that water penetrates the entire root system and drains freely from the bottom of the pot.

- Avoid overhead watering or soaking the foliage, as this can promote fungal diseases and rot. Instead, water orchids at the base of the plant, directly onto the growing medium.

4. Soaking vs. Dunking:

    - Consider soaking or dunking orchid pots in a container of water to ensure thorough hydration. Submerge the pot in water for 10-15 minutes, allowing the growing medium to absorb moisture fully. Drain excess water from the pot after soaking.

    - Alternatively, use the "pour-through" method by watering orchids until water flows freely from the drainage holes, ensuring complete saturation of the growing medium.

5. Humidity and Evaporation:

- Adjust watering frequency based on humidity levels and evaporation rates in your growing environment. Higher humidity levels and increased airflow may require less frequent watering, while lower humidity levels and drier conditions may necessitate more frequent watering.

6. Observation and Monitoring:

- Monitor orchids regularly for signs of dehydration or overwatering, such as wilted leaves, yellowing or browning of foliage, or mushy, blackened roots.

- Adjust your watering routine based on your orchids' response and environmental conditions, aiming to maintain a balance between

hydration and aeration for
healthy root growth.

Mastering orchid watering techniques and providing consistent, appropriate moisture levels, you can ensure the health, vigor, and vitality of your orchids, leading to vibrant blooms and lush foliage. Pay attention to your orchids' individual needs and environmental conditions, and adjust your watering routine accordingly for optimal results.

CHAPTER 5

Potting and Repotting

5.1 Signs Your Orchid Needs Repotting

Knowing when to repot your orchid is essential for maintaining its health and promoting optimal growth. While orchids generally prefer to be slightly pot-bound, there are several signs that indicate it's time to repot your orchid:

1. Overcrowded Roots:

    - When you notice that the orchid's roots have filled the pot completely and are tightly packed, it's a clear indication that the plant has outgrown its current container. Overcrowded roots can lead to poor drainage, air circulation, and nutrient uptake, which can negatively impact the orchid's health and growth.

2. Soggy or Decomposing Growing Medium:

    - If the orchid's growing medium has broken down, become waterlogged, or developed a sour odor, it's time to repot. Decomposing growing medium can lead to root rot, fungal infections, and other issues that compromise the orchid's root system and overall health.

3. Stunted Growth or Declining Health:

    - When an orchid exhibits stunted growth, yellowing or wilting leaves, or a decline in overall health and vigor, it may indicate root congestion or nutrient depletion in the potting medium. Repotting allows you to refresh the growing medium, provide

additional space for root
growth, and address any
underlying issues affecting
the orchid's health.

4. Lack of Flowering:

- If your orchid has stopped
  blooming or produces fewer
  flowers than usual, it may be
  a sign that it needs repotting.
  Over time, the accumulation
  of salts, minerals, and organic
  matter in the potting medium
  can interfere with nutrient
  uptake and flowering.
  Repotting can rejuvenate the
  orchid's root system and
  stimulate blooming.

5. Potting Medium Breakdown:

- Orchid potting mediums,
  such as bark, sphagnum
  moss, or coconut husk chips,
  break down over time as they
  decompose or compact.
  When the potting medium

breaks down, it loses its
ability to provide adequate
aeration, drainage, and
moisture retention for healthy
root growth. Repotting allows
you to replace the old potting
medium with fresh, clean
material.

6. Excessive Algae or Moss Growth:

- If you notice excessive algae
  or moss growth on the
  surface of the potting
  medium, it may indicate that
  the medium is breaking down
  or retaining too much
  moisture. Algae and moss
  can compete with orchid
  roots for nutrients and
  oxygen, leading to root
  suffocation and poor growth.
  Repotting can help eliminate
  algae or moss infestations
  and create a healthier
  growing environment for the
  orchid.

7. Potting Mix Decomposition:

- Orchid potting mixes degrade over time, becoming compacted, acidic, or waterlogged. If you observe that the potting mix has broken down into fine particles or lost its structure, it's time to repot. Freshening up the potting mix ensures proper aeration, drainage, and nutrient availability for healthy root growth.

When repotting your orchid, choose a clean, appropriately sized pot with good drainage, and use fresh potting medium tailored to the orchid's specific needs. Handle the orchid's roots carefully during repotting to avoid damage, and provide optimal care and growing conditions to help the orchid adjust to its new environment. By recognizing the signs that your orchid needs repotting and taking timely action, you can ensure the continued health and vitality of your prized plant.

5.2 Steps for Repotting Orchids

Repotting orchids is an essential task to maintain their health and vitality. Follow these steps to repot your orchid successfully:

1. Prepare Your Materials:

    - Gather all necessary materials, including a clean pot with drainage holes, fresh potting mix suitable for orchids, pruning shears or scissors, and gloves if desired.

2. Choose the Right Time:

    - Plan to repot your orchid during its active growing season, typically in spring or early summer, when new growth is emerging. Avoid repotting while the orchid is in bloom or undergoing significant stress, as this can

impact flowering and
recovery.

3. Water the Orchid:

- Water the orchid thoroughly
  a day or two before repotting
  to hydrate the roots and make
  them more pliable. Moist
  roots are less likely to break
  during repotting, reducing
  stress on the plant.

4. Remove the Orchid from Its Pot:

- Carefully remove the orchid
  from its current pot by gently
  grasping the base of the plant
  and tipping the pot to loosen
  the root ball. If the roots are
  tightly packed, gently tease
  them apart with your fingers
  or a wooden stick to loosen
  the root mass.

5. Inspect the Roots:

- Examine the orchid's roots
  for signs of rot, damage, or

overcrowding. Trim away
any dead, mushy, or brown
roots using sterilized pruning
shears or scissors. Healthy
roots are firm, plump, and
white or green in color.

6. Prepare the New Pot:

    - Choose a clean pot that is
      slightly larger than the
      orchid's root system to allow
      for future growth. Ensure the
      pot has drainage holes to
      prevent waterlogging. Add a
      layer of fresh orchid potting
      mix to the bottom of the pot
      to provide a stable base for
      the orchid.

7. Repot the Orchid:

    - Position the orchid in the
      center of the new pot,
      spreading out the roots
      evenly. Add fresh potting
      mix around the roots, gently
      pressing it down to provide

support. Ensure the orchid's pseudobulbs or base of the stem are at the same level as they were in the previous pot.

8. Water and Settle the Orchid:

    - Water the orchid lightly to settle the potting mix around the roots and remove any air pockets. Avoid overwatering immediately after repotting, as this can lead to root suffocation or rot. Allow the orchid to drain thoroughly before returning it to its usual growing location.

9. Provide Care and Monitoring:

    - Place the repotted orchid in a suitable location with appropriate light, temperature, and humidity levels. Monitor the orchid closely in the days and weeks following repotting, adjusting care as needed to help the

plant acclimate to its new
environment.

10. Maintain Regular Care:

- Continue to provide proper care,
  including watering, fertilizing, and
  grooming, to support the orchid's
  recovery and growth. Avoid
  disturbing the orchid unnecessarily
  and allow it time to establish its roots
  in the new potting medium.

Following these steps for repotting orchids,
you can ensure a smooth transition and
promote the health and vitality of your
prized plants. Remember to be patient and
gentle during the repotting process, and
provide optimal care to help your orchid
thrive in its new home.

5.3 Choosing the Correct Potting Mix

Choosing the correct potting mix is crucial
for the health and well-being of your
orchids, as it provides essential support,

aeration, moisture retention, and nutrient uptake for healthy root growth. There are several types of potting mixes available for orchids, each with its unique characteristics and suitability for different orchid species and growing conditions. Here are some popular options:

1. Orchid Bark Mix:

    - Orchid bark mix is one of the most commonly used potting mixes for orchids, especially epiphytic species such as Phalaenopsis, Cattleya, and Oncidium. Orchid bark consists of large chunks of bark from various tree species, providing excellent drainage, aeration, and stability for orchid roots.

2. Sphagnum Moss Mix:

    - Sphagnum moss mix is prized for its moisture retention properties, making it ideal for orchids that require high humidity levels, such as Paphiopedilum, Phragmipedium, and Masdevallia. Sphagnum moss retains water well while allowing for good airflow and root development.

3. Coconut Husk Chips Mix:

- Coconut husk chips mix, also known as coco chips or coir, is derived from the fibrous outer husk of coconuts. Coconut husk chips provide excellent drainage, aeration, and moisture retention, making them suitable for a wide range of orchids, including Cattleya, Dendrobium, and Vanda.

4. Perlite and Charcoal Mix:

- Perlite and charcoal mix is a lightweight and porous potting mix that improves drainage and aeration while preventing compaction and root suffocation. Perlite and charcoal mix are often used as components in custom orchid potting mixes, providing additional structure and stability.

5. Specialty Orchid Mixes:

- Specialty orchid mixes tailored to specific orchid species or growing conditions are available commercially and may contain a combination of ingredients such as bark, sphagnum moss, coconut husk chips, perlite, and charcoal. These mixes are formulated to meet the unique needs of orchids and provide optimal growing conditions for healthy growth and blooming.

When choosing a potting mix for your orchids, consider factors such as the orchid species, growing environment, watering frequency, and cultural preferences. Experiment with different mixes and combinations to find the optimal blend for your orchids' needs. Remember to repot your orchids every 1-2 years to refresh the potting mix and promote healthy root growth and blooming. By selecting the correct potting mix and providing optimal growing conditions, you can ensure the health, vigor, and vitality of your orchids for years to come.

CHAPTER 6

Orchid Pests and Diseases

6.1 Common Pests Affecting Orchids

Orchids, like any other plants, are susceptible to various pests that can affect their health and vitality. Identifying and addressing pest infestations promptly is crucial for preventing damage and maintaining the beauty of your orchids. Here are some common pests that can affect orchids:

1. Aphids (Aphidoidea):

    - Aphids are small, soft-bodied insects that feed on the sap of orchid leaves, stems, and flower buds. They reproduce rapidly and can cause distorted growth, yellowing leaves, and premature bud drop. Aphids also excrete honeydew, attracting ants and promoting the growth of sooty mold.

2. Scale Insects (Coccoidea):

    - Scale insects are small, oval-shaped pests that attach themselves to orchid leaves, pseudobulbs, or stems, where they feed on plant sap. They produce a waxy covering that protects them from predators and pesticides. Heavy scale infestations can weaken orchids and lead to leaf yellowing, stunted growth, and dieback.

3. Spider Mites (Tetranychidae):

    - Spider mites are tiny arachnids that feed on orchid leaves by piercing plant cells and sucking out the contents. They typically cause

stippling or yellowing of
leaves, fine webbing on the
undersides of leaves, and leaf
drop. Spider mites thrive in
dry, dusty conditions and can
multiply rapidly, especially in
warm weather.

4. Mealybugs (Pseudococcidae):

- Mealybugs are small, soft-
bodied insects covered in a
white, powdery wax coating.
They feed on orchid tissue by
inserting their piercing
mouthparts into plant cells
and sucking out the sap.
Mealybug infestations can
lead to stunted growth,
yellowing leaves, and the
development of mold or
fungal diseases.

5. Thrips (Thysanoptera):

- Thrips are slender, winged
insects that feed on orchid
flowers, buds, and young

foliage. They pierce plant tissue and suck out the sap, causing distorted growth, brown streaks or spots on flowers, and premature flower drop. Thrips can also transmit viruses from infected plants to healthy ones.

6. Snails and Slugs (Gastropoda):

    - Snails and slugs are nocturnal pests that feed on orchid leaves, flowers, and tender shoots. They leave behind ragged holes or chewed edges on foliage, as well as slime trails. Snail and slug damage is more common in humid environments or during periods of high rainfall.

7. Fungus Gnats (Sciaridae):

    - Fungus gnats are small, black flies that lay their eggs in moist potting medium. The larvae feed on organic matter and plant roots, causing root damage and predisposing orchids to root rot and fungal diseases. Adult fungus gnats are nuisance pests that can be found flying around orchid pots.

8. Orchid Weevils (Epicauta spp.):

- Orchid weevils are beetles that feed on orchid flowers, buds, and new growth. They chew irregular holes in flowers and cause petals to deform or drop prematurely. Orchid weevil larvae also tunnel into pseudobulbs, causing internal damage and weakening the plant.

To prevent and manage pest infestations in orchids, practice good cultural practices such as maintaining proper sanitation, providing adequate airflow, and avoiding overwatering. Monitor orchids regularly for signs of pests, and treat infestations promptly using appropriate methods such as insecticidal soap, neem oil, or biological controls. When using pesticides, always follow label instructions and use caution to minimize harm to beneficial insects and the environment. By staying vigilant and proactive, you can protect your orchids from pests and ensure their continued health and beauty.

6.2 Recognizing Orchid Diseases

Orchids are susceptible to various diseases caused by fungi, bacteria, viruses, and environmental factors. Identifying and addressing these diseases promptly is essential for maintaining the health and vigor of your orchids. Here are some common orchid diseases and their symptoms:

1. Root Rot:

   - Root rot is a fungal disease caused by overwatering, poor

drainage, or contaminated potting medium. Symptoms include mushy, blackened roots, wilting or yellowing leaves, and a foul odor emanating from the potting medium. Severe root rot can lead to plant death if left untreated.

2. Leaf Spot:

    - Leaf spot is a fungal or bacterial disease characterized by small, dark lesions or spots on orchid leaves. These spots may enlarge and merge, leading to leaf yellowing, browning, or defoliation. Leaf spot diseases are often caused by high humidity, poor air circulation, or overhead watering.

3. Botrytis Blight:

- Botrytis blight, also known as gray mold, is a fungal disease that affects orchid flowers, buds, and foliage. It appears as fuzzy, grayish-brown mold on flowers, stems, or leaves, especially in humid conditions. Botrytis blight can cause flower buds to rot and drop prematurely.

4. Crown Rot:

- Crown rot is a fungal disease that affects the growing point or crown of orchids, leading to soft, mushy tissue and eventual collapse of the plant. It is often caused by overwatering, poor ventilation, or damage to the crown tissue. Infected orchids may exhibit wilting, yellowing, or browning of leaves.

5. Virus Diseases:

- Orchid viruses are systemic diseases that can cause various symptoms, including leaf mottling, streaking, distortion, or necrosis, as well as abnormal flower coloration or patterning. Virus-infected orchids may exhibit reduced vigor, stunted growth, and decreased flowering. Once a plant is infected with a virus, there is no cure, and infected plants should be isolated and discarded to prevent spread to other orchids.

6. Fusarium Wilt:

- Fusarium wilt is a fungal disease that affects the vascular system of orchids, causing wilting, yellowing, and collapse of leaves. Infected plants may exhibit brown streaks or discoloration in the stems or pseudobulbs. Fusarium wilt

is often spread through
contaminated potting medium
or tools.

7. Bacterial Soft Rot:

    - Bacterial soft rot is a
      bacterial disease that affects
      orchid pseudobulbs, leaves,
      or flowers, causing soft,
      water-soaked lesions that
      quickly turn mushy and
      slimy. The affected tissue
      may emit a foul odor, and the
      infection can spread rapidly
      throughout the plant if not
      treated promptly.

8. Physiological Disorders:

    - Orchids may also experience
      physiological disorders
      caused by environmental
      stressors such as temperature
      extremes, improper watering,
      or inadequate light.
      Symptoms include leaf

yellowing, leaf tip dieback, or abnormal growth patterns.

To manage orchid diseases effectively, it's essential to practice good cultural practices such as proper watering, adequate ventilation, and sanitation. Remove and discard diseased plant parts promptly to prevent the spread of pathogens. Treat infections with appropriate fungicides, bactericides, or antiviral agents as recommended by horticultural professionals.

6.3 Preventative Measures and Treatments

Preventing and managing orchid diseases requires a combination of proactive measures and targeted treatments to maintain the health and vitality of your plants. Here are some preventative measures and treatments for common orchid diseases:

1. Cultural Practices:

    - Maintain proper cultural practices, including providing

adequate airflow, avoiding
overwatering, and
maintaining proper humidity
levels, to create an
environment that is less
conducive to disease
development.

2. Sanitation:

- Practice good sanitation by
  regularly cleaning and
  disinfecting tools, pots, and
  growing areas to prevent the
  spread of pathogens. Remove
  and discard diseased plant
  parts promptly to prevent the
  spread of infection.

3. Quarantine:

- Quarantine new orchids for a
  few weeks before introducing
  them to your collection to
  monitor for signs of disease.
  Keep new plants separate
  from healthy orchids to

prevent potential
contamination.

4. Watering Practices:

- Water orchids carefully to
  avoid overwatering, which
  can lead to root rot and other
  fungal diseases. Water in the
  morning to allow foliage to
  dry quickly and reduce the
  risk of fungal infections.

5. Fungicides and Bactericides:

- Apply fungicides or
  bactericides preventatively or
  as directed at the first sign of
  disease to prevent further
  spread. Choose products
  labeled for orchids and
  follow label instructions
  carefully.

6. Virus Testing and Elimination:

- Test orchids for viruses using
  specialized diagnostic tools
  and techniques available

through laboratories or professional services. If a plant tests positive for a virus, consider removing and discarding it to prevent spread to other orchids.

7. Isolation and Quarantine:

   - Isolate infected orchids from healthy plants to prevent the spread of disease. Place infected plants in a separate location and avoid using the same tools or equipment on healthy plants without proper disinfection.

8. Environmental Management:

   - Manage environmental conditions such as temperature, humidity, and light levels to create an optimal growing environment for orchids and reduce stress that can predispose plants to disease.

9. Biological Controls:

- Consider using biological controls such as beneficial insects, predatory mites, or microbial agents to suppress pest populations and prevent infestations. Biological controls can be effective alternatives to chemical pesticides.

10. Regular Monitoring:

- Monitor orchids regularly for signs of disease, including changes in growth, appearance, or behavior. Early detection allows for prompt treatment and prevents the spread of infection to other plants.

CHAPTER 7

Advanced Orchid Care Techniques

7.1 Orchid Propagation Methods

Orchid propagation allows enthusiasts to expand their collections, share plants with others, and preserve rare or valuable orchid species. While some orchids can be propagated from seeds, many orchid enthusiasts prefer vegetative propagation methods, which involve reproducing orchids from existing plant material such as pseudobulbs, divisions, keikis, or backbulbs. Here are several advanced orchid propagation methods:

1. Division:

   - Division is one of the most common methods of propagating orchids, particularly sympodial orchids with pseudobulbs, such as Cattleya, Dendrobium, and Oncidium species. To divide an orchid, carefully separate the rhizome or pseudobulbs into sections, ensuring each division has healthy roots and sufficient growing points. Plant the divisions in individual pots with fresh potting mix, and provide optimal growing conditions to encourage new root and shoot growth.

2. Keikis:

- Keikis are miniature plantlets that develop along the flower spike or aerial roots of certain orchid species, such as Phalaenopsis and Dendrobium. Keikis can be encouraged to develop by providing high humidity, bright indirect light, and

adequate nutrition. Once the
keiki has developed several
roots and leaves, it can be
carefully detached from the
parent plant and potted
separately to grow into a new
orchid.

3. Backbulbs:

- Backbulbs are dormant or
  mature pseudobulbs that can
  be used to propagate
  sympodial orchids. When
  repotting orchids, save any
  healthy backbulbs that have
  viable buds or growing
  points. Plant the backbulbs in
  individual pots with fresh
  potting mix, and provide
  appropriate care to encourage
  new growth and root
  development. Backbulbs may
  take longer to establish than
  divisions but can eventually
  produce new shoots and
  flower spikes.

4. Tissue Culture:

- Tissue culture, also known as micropropagation, is an advanced propagation technique used to produce large numbers of orchid clones under sterile laboratory conditions. Tissue culture involves culturing small pieces of orchid tissue, such as meristems or protocorms, in a nutrient-rich agar medium supplemented with growth hormones. Once the tissue cultures have developed into plantlets, they can be transferred to soil or agar plugs and grown into mature orchids.

5. Meristem Culture:

- Meristem culture is a specialized form of tissue culture that involves culturing the meristematic tissue found at the growing tips of orchid shoots or roots. Meristem culture allows for the production of disease-free orchid clones and can be used to propagate orchids that are difficult to propagate by other methods. Meristem culture requires highly sterile conditions and specialized equipment but can yield genetically identical orchid plants with desirable traits.

6. Seed Propagation:

- Seed propagation is the traditional method of reproducing orchids but is more challenging and time-consuming than vegetative propagation methods. Orchid seeds are tiny and dust-like, requiring sterile conditions and specialized techniques to germinate and grow into mature plants. Seed propagation allows for the production of genetically diverse orchids and can be used to create new hybrids or preserve rare species.

7.2 Pruning and Trimming

Pruning and trimming are essential orchid care techniques that help maintain plant health, promote new growth, and enhance the aesthetic appeal of orchids. While orchids generally require minimal pruning compared to other plants, occasional trimming of dead, damaged, or overgrown plant parts can benefit their overall growth and appearance. Here are some tips for pruning and trimming orchids:

1. Remove Dead or Dying Leaves:

   - Regularly inspect your orchids for dead or yellowing leaves, which can detract from the plant's appearance and potentially harbor pests or diseases. Use sterilized pruning shears or scissors to carefully trim away dead or

dying leaves at the base of
the plant.

2. Trim Overgrown Roots:

- Orchids may produce aerial
  roots that grow excessively
  long or become tangled over
  time. Trim back overgrown
  roots using clean, sharp
  scissors, leaving about an
  inch of healthy root tissue
  attached to the plant. Avoid
  cutting healthy roots
  unnecessarily, as they play a
  vital role in nutrient uptake
  and anchoring the plant.

3. Prune Flower Spikes:

- After orchid flowers have
  faded and dropped, trim back
  the flower spike to encourage
  new growth and prevent the
  plant from expending energy
  on producing seeds. Use
  sterilized pruning shears to
  cut the flower spike just

above a node or pseudobulb, taking care not to damage surrounding plant tissue.

4. Remove Spent Pseudobulbs:

    • Some orchid species, such as Cattleyas and Dendrobiums, produce pseudobulbs that may eventually become shriveled or spent. Remove old or spent pseudobulbs using sterilized pruning shears to encourage the plant to focus its energy on producing new growth and flowering.

5. Prune Diseased or Infected Tissue:

    • If you notice signs of disease or infection on your orchid, such as fungal spots, bacterial lesions, or rotting tissue, promptly prune away the affected plant parts to prevent further spread. Make clean cuts using sterilized tools, and dispose of the infected material carefully to avoid contaminating other plants.

6. Trim Orchid Mounts:

- If you grow orchids mounted on bark, cork, or other substrates, periodically trim back any moss, algae, or debris that accumulates on the mount. Use scissors or a sharp knife to carefully remove excess growth, taking care not to damage the orchid's roots or pseudobulbs.

7. Prune for Aesthetic Purposes:

- Prune orchids for aesthetic purposes to maintain a tidy appearance and encourage balanced growth. Remove leggy or straggly growth, reshape unruly plants, and thin out crowded areas to improve airflow and light penetration.

When pruning or trimming orchids, always use clean, sharp tools to minimize the risk of injury and infection. Sterilize pruning shears or scissors with rubbing alcohol or a bleach solution before and after each use to prevent the spread of pathogens. Take care to make clean cuts at the appropriate angle to minimize damage to the plant and promote rapid healing. With proper pruning and trimming techniques, you can keep your orchids looking their best and promote healthy growth and flowering.

7.3 Orchid Mounting

Mounting orchids is a popular alternative to traditional potting methods, allowing orchids to grow attached to a variety of natural or artificial substrates such as bark, cork, tree fern, or driftwood. Orchid mounting replicates the epiphytic growing conditions found in the orchids' native habitats, providing good airflow, drainage, and exposure to light. Here's how to mount orchids effectively:

1. Select a Suitable Mount:

    - Choose a mount that is porous, sturdy, and able to retain moisture without becoming waterlogged. Common mounting materials include tree fern plaques, cork bark, hardwood branches, or driftwood. Ensure the mount is appropriately sized for the orchid's root system and growth habit.

2. Prepare the Mount:

    - Soak the mount in water to hydrate it thoroughly and remove any dust or debris. If using tree fern plaques or cork bark, soak them overnight to ensure they are fully saturated and pliable.

3. Attach the Orchid:

    - Carefully position the orchid on the mount, taking care to arrange the roots evenly and securely. Use nylon fishing line, cotton thread, or twist ties to anchor the orchid to the mount, wrapping the material around the roots and pseudobulbs without constricting them.

4. Secure the Orchid:

- Secure the orchid firmly to the mount, ensuring it is stable and will not shift or fall off during watering or handling. Avoid using materials that may degrade or rot over time, such as metal wire or rubber bands.

5. Provide Support:

- If the orchid is top-heavy or unstable on the mount, provide additional support by adding stakes, clips, or ties to hold it in place. Use materials that are gentle on the plant and will not damage the roots or pseudobulbs.

6. Hang or Display the Mounted Orchid:

    - Hang the mounted orchid in a suitable location with appropriate light, temperature, and humidity levels. Consider mounting orchids in a greenhouse, on a patio, or under a shaded tree where they can receive filtered sunlight and good airflow.

7. Water and Maintain:

    - Water mounted orchids by misting or soaking the mount regularly to keep the roots hydrated. Monitor the moisture level carefully to prevent the mount from drying out completely or becoming waterlogged. Fertilize mounted orchids periodically with a diluted orchid fertilizer to provide essential nutrients for healthy growth and flowering.

8. Monitor Growth and Adjust as Needed:

    - Monitor the growth of the mounted orchid regularly and adjust its position or support as needed to accommodate new growth and prevent overcrowding. Check for signs of root rot, dehydration, or pests, and address any issues promptly to maintain the health and vitality of the orchid.

Mounting orchids allows enthusiasts to create stunning displays of orchids in naturalistic settings, such as terrariums, vivariums, or botanical gardens. Experiment with different mounting materials and techniques to find the best option for your orchids' needs and preferences. With proper care and attention, mounted orchids can

thrive and reward growers with beautiful
blooms and healthy growth.

CHAPTER 8

Orchid Display and Presentation

8.1 Creating Stunning Orchid Displays

Creating stunning orchid displays is an art form that allows enthusiasts to showcase the beauty and diversity of orchids in captivating arrangements. Whether you're planning a formal exhibition, designing a home garden, or arranging a centerpiece for a special event, thoughtful consideration of layout, composition, and presentation can elevate your orchid display to breathtaking heights. Here are some tips for creating stunning orchid displays:

1. Choose a Focal Point:

    - Select a focal point or central feature for your orchid display, such as a large specimen orchid, a cascading flower arrangement, or a decorative vase or pedestal. The focal point anchors the display and draws the viewer's attention, serving as the centerpiece around which other orchids are arranged.

2. Consider Scale and Proportion:

    - Pay attention to scale and proportion when arranging orchids, ensuring that the size and shape of individual plants complement each other and the overall composition. Use a variety of orchid species, sizes, and growth habits to create visual interest and balance in the display.

3. Mix Colors and Textures:

    - Experiment with a diverse range of orchid colors, patterns, and textures to create dynamic contrasts and

harmonious combinations.
Mix bold, vibrant blooms
with delicate, pastel shades,
and pair smooth, glossy
leaves with textured, velvety
foliage for visual impact.

4. Incorporate Complementary
   Elements:

   - Enhance your orchid display
     with complementary
     elements such as decorative
     containers, natural accents, or
     ornamental accessories.
     Consider incorporating rocks,
     driftwood, moss, or
     decorative stones to create a
     naturalistic setting that
     complements the orchids'
     beauty.

5. Arrange Orchids in Layers:

   - Arrange orchids in layers or
     tiers to create depth and
     dimensionality in your
     display. Place taller orchids

toward the back or center of
the arrangement and shorter
orchids toward the front or
edges to create visual interest
and perspective.

6. Pay Attention to Symmetry and
   Balance:

   - Strive for symmetry and
     balance in your orchid
     display, arranging orchids
     and other elements in a
     harmonious and visually
     pleasing manner. Use
     asymmetrical compositions to
     create dynamic tension and
     movement, but maintain
     overall balance and cohesion
     in the arrangement.

7. Experiment with Different Display
   Techniques:

   - Explore different display
     techniques and presentation
     styles to showcase orchids in
     creative and innovative ways.

Consider hanging orchids
from ceilings or walls,
arranging them in terrariums
or glass containers, or
creating living sculptures and
installations that capture the
imagination.

8. Provide Proper Lighting and
    Environment:

    - Ensure that your orchid
      display receives adequate
      lighting and environmental
      conditions to promote healthy
      growth and blooming. Place
      the display in a location with
      bright, indirect light, and
      maintain optimal
      temperature, humidity, and
      airflow to prolong the
      longevity of the flowers and
      foliage.

9. Maintain and Refresh the Display:

    - Regularly maintain and
      refresh your orchid display

by removing faded blooms, trimming dead foliage, and replacing spent orchids with fresh specimens. Keep the display clean and tidy, and monitor orchids for signs of pests, diseases, or stress, addressing any issues promptly to preserve the beauty of the arrangement.

10. Share Your Passion for Orchids:

- Share your passion for orchids with others by inviting friends, family, or fellow enthusiasts to admire your stunning orchid display. Host orchid-themed events, workshops, or garden tours to inspire others and foster a sense of community among orchid lovers.

8.2 Orchid Photography Tips

Orchids are some of the most photogenic plants, with their intricate blooms and vibrant colors captivating photographers around the world. Capturing stunning orchid photos requires careful attention to composition, lighting, and camera settings. Whether you're photographing orchids in a greenhouse, garden, or orchid show, these tips will help you take beautiful orchid photos:

1. Use Natural Light:

    - Whenever possible, photograph orchids in natural light to showcase their true colors and delicate details. Choose a bright, overcast day or position the orchids near a window to take advantage of soft, diffused light that minimizes harsh shadows and highlights.

2. Control Background:

- Pay attention to the background when composing your orchid photos, ensuring it is clean, uncluttered, and complementary to the subject. Use a solid-colored backdrop or position the orchids against foliage, sky, or other natural elements to create a visually appealing composition.

3. Experiment with Angles:

- Explore different angles and perspectives when photographing orchids to capture their beauty from unique viewpoints. Get down low to shoot orchids at eye level or experiment with overhead shots to showcase the intricate patterns and textures of the flowers and foliage.

4. Focus on Details:

- Use a macro lens or macro mode on your camera to capture close-up shots of orchid blooms, revealing their intricate details and textures. Focus on the central part of the flower, such as the lip or column, to highlight its unique features and characteristics.

5. Consider Depth of Field:

   - Adjust the aperture settings on your camera to control the depth of field in your orchid photos. Use a wide aperture (low f-stop) to create a shallow depth of field, blurring the background and drawing attention to the orchid's focal point. Alternatively, use a narrow aperture (high f-stop) to keep more of the scene in focus.

6. Use Tripod and Remote Shutter Release:

- To minimize camera shake and ensure sharp, clear photos, use a tripod to stabilize your camera and a remote shutter release or self-timer function to trigger the shutter without touching the camera. This is especially important when shooting in low light or using slow shutter speeds.

7. Experiment with Composition:

- Explore different composition techniques, such as the rule of thirds, leading lines, and negative space, to create visually dynamic orchid photos. Experiment with framing, cropping, and perspective to create compelling compositions that draw the viewer's eye to the focal point.

8. Pay Attention to White Balance:

- Adjust the white balance settings on your camera to accurately capture the colors of the orchids under different lighting conditions. Use the auto white balance mode for natural light or experiment with custom white balance settings to achieve accurate color reproduction.

9. Be Patient and Observant:

- Take your time when photographing orchids, observing their behavior, movement, and natural surroundings. Be patient and wait for the perfect moment to capture the beauty of the orchids in bloom, taking multiple shots from different angles and settings to ensure you get the perfect shot.

10. Experiment and Have Fun:

- Don't be afraid to experiment with different techniques, settings, and creative ideas when photographing orchids. Embrace the creative process, try new things, and have fun capturing the stunning beauty of these extraordinary flowers.

8.3 Orchid Show Participation

Participating in orchid shows is an exciting opportunity for orchid enthusiasts to share their passion, learn from fellow growers, and showcase their prized orchid collections to a wider audience. Whether you're a seasoned exhibitor or a novice hobbyist, participating in orchid shows can be a rewarding and enriching experience. Here are some tips for getting involved in orchid shows:

1. Research Orchid Shows:

- Research upcoming orchid shows in your area or region, and identify events that align with your interests, schedule, and level of experience. Explore local orchid societies, botanical gardens, or horticultural organizations that host orchid shows and exhibitions.

2. Plan Ahead:

- Plan ahead and prepare your orchid collection for exhibition well in advance of the show date. Select healthy, well-grown orchids that are in peak bloom or condition, and carefully groom and prepare them for display.

3. Register and Submit Entries:

- Register for the orchid show and submit your entries according to the show's guidelines and deadlines.

Complete entry forms, labels, and documentation accurately, and follow any specific requirements for plant staging, labeling, or presentation.

4. Arrange Orchids for Display:

    *   Arrange your orchids for display in an attractive and eye-catching manner, paying attention to layout, composition, and visual appeal. Group similar orchids together, vary heights and textures, and use props or accessories to enhance the overall presentation.

5. Provide Care and Maintenance:

    *   Provide proper care and maintenance for your orchids throughout the duration of the show, ensuring they remain hydrated, well-lit, and free from pests or diseases.

Monitor orchids for signs of stress, wilting, or damage, and address any issues promptly to maintain their health and appearance.

6. Engage with Visitors:

- Engage with visitors, fellow exhibitors, and orchid enthusiasts at the show, sharing your knowledge, experiences, and enthusiasm for orchids. Be prepared to answer questions, provide advice, and offer insights into orchid culture, care, and cultivation.

7. Attend Educational Programs:

- Take advantage of educational programs, workshops, and seminars offered at the orchid show to expand your knowledge and skills. Attend lectures, demonstrations, or hands-on activities led by experienced growers, experts, and industry professionals.

8. Network and Learn:

    - Network with other orchid enthusiasts, growers, and vendors at the show, building relationships and connections within the orchid community. Exchange ideas, tips, and resources, and learn from others' experiences and expertise.

9. Enjoy the Experience:

    - Enjoy the experience of participating in the orchid show, celebrating the beauty and diversity of orchids with fellow enthusiasts and visitors. Take pride in your orchid collection and the effort you've put into preparing for the show, and celebrate the joy of sharing your passion with others.

10. Reflect and Improve:

- After the show, take time to reflect on your experience and evaluate your performance as an exhibitor. Identify areas for improvement, gather feedback from judges or peers, and make adjustments or changes to your approach for future shows.

Participating in orchid shows offers a unique opportunity to connect with fellow orchid enthusiasts, showcase your orchid collection, and celebrate the beauty and diversity of orchids. Whether you're a hobbyist grower, a seasoned exhibitor, or a curious observer, orchid shows provide a wealth of inspiration, knowledge, and camaraderie for all who share a love for these extraordinary plants.

CHAPTER 9

Troubleshooting

9.1 Identifying Orchid Problems

Identifying orchid problems can be challenging, as symptoms of stress, disease, or environmental issues may vary depending on the species and growing conditions. However, careful observation and attention to detail can help you pinpoint the cause of your orchid's distress. Here are some common orchid problems and their associated symptoms:

1. Overwatering:

     - Symptoms: Yellowing or wilting leaves, mushy or rotting roots, foul odor emanating from the potting medium, mold or fungal growth on the surface of the potting mix.

- Cause: Excessive moisture in the potting medium, poor drainage, or inadequate airflow around the roots.

- Solution: Allow the potting mix to dry out between waterings, improve drainage by repotting in a well-draining medium, and ensure adequate airflow around the roots.

2. Underwatering:

   - Symptoms: Wrinkled or shriveled leaves, limp or floppy growth, dry and desiccated roots, leaf tips turning brown or crispy.

   - Cause: Insufficient moisture in the potting medium, infrequent watering, or environmental conditions that promote rapid evaporation.

   - Solution: Water orchids thoroughly when the potting

mix is dry to the touch, adjust watering frequency based on environmental conditions, and consider increasing humidity around the plant.

3. Sunburn:

- Symptoms: Yellowing or bleaching of leaves, brown or black spots on foliage, scorched or crispy leaf edges, wilting or drooping growth.

- Cause: Excessive exposure to direct sunlight, especially during the hottest part of the day, without adequate protection or acclimatization.

- Solution: Move orchids to a location with filtered or indirect sunlight, provide shade during the hottest hours of the day, and gradually acclimate plants to brighter light levels.

4. Temperature Stress:

- Symptoms: Leaf discoloration or burning, wilting or drooping growth, slowed or stunted growth, premature bud drop or flower fading.

- Cause: Extreme temperatures, temperature fluctuations, or exposure to drafts or cold drafts.

- Solution: Maintain stable temperatures within the optimal range for your orchid species, protect plants from cold drafts or sudden temperature changes, and provide supplemental heating or cooling as needed.

5. Nutrient Deficiency:

- Symptoms: Yellowing or chlorosis of leaves, poor growth or blooming, weak or spindly stems, distorted or abnormal growth patterns.

- Cause: Lack of essential
  nutrients such as nitrogen,
  phosphorus, potassium, or
  micronutrients in the potting
  medium or water supply.

- Solution: Fertilize orchids
  regularly with a balanced
  orchid fertilizer, adjust the
  fertilizer formulation based
  on plant needs and growth
  stage, and monitor for signs
  of nutrient deficiency or
  excess.

6. Pest Infestations:

- Symptoms: Visible pests
  such as aphids, scale insects,
  spider mites, or mealybugs
  on leaves, stems, or flower
  buds, distorted growth,
  stippling or discoloration of
  leaves, fine webbing or mold
  on foliage.

- Cause: Infestation by insects, mites, or other pests that feed on orchid tissue or sap.

- Solution: Inspect orchids regularly for signs of pest activity, treat infestations promptly with appropriate insecticides, horticultural oils, or biological controls, and quarantine affected plants to prevent spread to other orchids.

7. Disease:

- Symptoms: Leaf spots or lesions, rotting or discolored roots, wilting or collapsing growth, fungal growth or mold on foliage or potting mix.

- Cause: Fungal, bacterial, or viral pathogens that infect orchid tissue and cause disease symptoms.

- Solution: Identify the underlying cause of the disease, improve growing conditions to promote plant health and vigor, and treat infections with appropriate fungicides, bactericides, or antiviral agents as recommended by experts.

8. Environmental Stress:

  - Symptoms: Leaf yellowing or dropping, wilting or drooping growth, reduced blooming or flowering, overall decline in plant health and vitality.

  - Cause: Exposure to environmental stressors such as extreme temperatures, low humidity, poor air circulation, or chemical exposure.

  - Solution: Identify and mitigate environmental stressors affecting orchids, provide optimal growing conditions, and minimize exposure to harmful chemicals or pollutants.

When diagnosing orchid problems, it's essential to consider all potential factors contributing to the plant's condition, including cultural practices, environmental conditions, and pest or disease pressures. Take a systematic approach to troubleshooting, starting with the most likely causes and ruling out other possibilities through careful observation and analysis. By identifying orchid problems early and taking appropriate corrective action, you can help your orchids thrive and flourish in their growing environment.

9.2 Solutions for Common Orchid Issues

Orchids are resilient plants, but they can still encounter various problems that affect their growth and appearance. Fortunately, many common orchid issues can be resolved with proper care, attention, and timely intervention. Here are solutions for addressing some common orchid problems:

1. Overwatering:

    - Solution: Allow the potting mix to dry out between waterings to prevent root rot and fungal infections. Adjust watering frequency based on environmental conditions and the specific needs of your orchid species. Ensure proper drainage by repotting orchids in a well-draining medium and avoid leaving orchids sitting in water-filled saucers.

2. Underwatering:

    - Solution: Water orchids thoroughly when the potting mix is dry to the touch, ensuring water penetrates the entire root system. Use a watering method that allows water to drain freely through

the potting medium and avoid
underwatering or allowing
orchids to become desiccated.

3. Sunburn:

    - Solution: Protect orchids
      from excessive sunlight by
      providing shade during the
      hottest part of the day or
      moving them to a location
      with filtered or indirect light.
      Acclimate orchids gradually
      to brighter light levels to
      prevent sunburn and leaf
      damage. Consider using sheer
      curtains, shade cloth, or
      blinds to filter sunlight and
      reduce intensity.

4. Temperature Stress:

    - Solution: Maintain stable
      temperatures within the
      optimal range for your orchid
      species, avoiding extremes or
      sudden fluctuations in
      temperature. Protect orchids

from cold drafts, hot air vents, or temperature differentials that can stress plants and compromise their health. Provide supplemental heating or cooling as needed to maintain ideal growing conditions.

5. Nutrient Deficiency:

- Solution: Fertilize orchids regularly with a balanced orchid fertilizer to provide essential nutrients for healthy growth and blooming. Adjust the fertilizer formulation based on plant needs, growth stage, and environmental conditions. Monitor for signs of nutrient deficiency or excess and adjust fertilization practices accordingly.

6. Pest Infestations:

- Solution: Inspect orchids regularly for signs of pest

activity, including visible insects, webs, or damage to foliage. Treat infestations promptly with appropriate insecticides, horticultural oils, or insecticidal soaps, following label instructions carefully. Quarantine affected plants to prevent the spread of pests to other orchids and monitor for recurrence.

7. Disease:

- Solution: Identify the underlying cause of orchid disease symptoms and treat infections with appropriate fungicides, bactericides, or antiviral agents as recommended by experts. Improve growing conditions to promote plant health and vigor, including proper watering, ventilation, and sanitation practices. Remove and dispose of infected plant material carefully to prevent further spread of disease.

8. Environmental Stress:

- Solution: Identify and mitigate environmental stressors affecting orchids, including extreme temperatures, low humidity, poor air circulation, or chemical exposure. Provide optimal growing conditions by adjusting lighting, temperature, humidity, and airflow to meet the needs of your orchid species. Minimize exposure to pollutants, chemicals, or harmful substances that may affect plant health.

When addressing orchid problems, it's essential to diagnose the underlying cause accurately and implement appropriate solutions tailored to the specific needs of your orchids. Monitor orchids closely for signs of improvement or recurrence, and adjust care practices as needed to promote plant health and vitality. By taking proactive steps to address common orchid issues and provide optimal growing conditions, you can help your orchids thrive and flourish in your care.